Deeper Secrets
of
Wealth Creation

Vincent Hope

TANZANIA EDUCATIONAL PUBLISHERS LTD

Tanzania Educational Publishers Ltd,
TEPU House,
Uganda road, Plot No. 45 Block MDA,
Telephone: +255 685 997583/ +255 758 147871
Email: tepultd@yahoo.com
Website: www.tepu.co.tz
P.O. Box 1222,
Bukoba, Tanzania.

ISBN 978-9987-07-063-3

Dedication

This book is dedicated to

God Almighty

for

Who Gave Me the Wisdom, Strength, Courage and

Perseverance To Navigate the Financial Storms of Life

and

Gain Valuable Financial Wisdom in the Process.

Contents

1. The Importance of Money

There is so much talk about money and rightfully so, because money seems to pervade every area of our lives.

When you wake up in the morning, have your bath and prepare yourself a nice breakfast, you cannot have it unless you have food to eat. You will only have food to eat if you purchased it; except of course if you are a farmer who grows your own food, and even at that, you cannot grow all you need and will still have to buy what you don't have.

To buy the food you don't have, you will need money. If you have a job, you will need to go the office after breakfast. If you must go to the office you must fill your car with gas. If you don't have a car you will have to take a bus to the office and still have to pay for your fare.

During the course of the day, you will need to make or receive calls. If you make calls, you will be charged for it. In this internet and social media age, you will definitely want to browse the internet, connect with friends and loved ones on Face book, Twitter and other social media platforms that will also cost you money.

During your lunch break, you must have it either alone or with a colleague.

And you will have to pay for it

After a day of hard work, you will as usual drive or take a cab home. When you get home, you will have supper. All these are not free – they cost money.

You also have weekly or monthly expenses to deal with. You will have to pay for electricity, heating, mortgage, insurance etc. If you have children in school, you have to pay tuition fees and if your children are still toddlers, you will still have to pay a nanny to look after them.

The use of money pervades every fabric of our lives. In the world today, a man or woman is judged successful based on the amount of money or financial resources he or she possess to take care of personal expenses with enough left to acquire luxury items and possibly give back to society.

2. So Why Money?

In the foregoing passage, the typical day of an individual is described. It shows what a person needs and must do to have a productive day.

God made us both as **independent** and **interdependent** beings. By being **independent** beings, we can think for ourselves, do things our own way and have our own things.

But no matter how independent we are, we still need the input of others to make our lives complete and worth living. If there is no need for other people, there will have been no need for procreation. Adam and Eve would have remained the only two human beings living on earth and if so, their influence on the earth would have remained minimal.

As **interdependent** beings we have needs that only other people can meet. There is no one on the surface of the planet that produces all he or she needs for living a good life.

No matter how wealthy a man is, he will not want to build a company just for the purpose of producing his own personal cars or private jets.

That will amount to a huge waste of his resources and time. He only simply needs to make an order for a car or private jet from **Teslar** or **Boeing**. If needs an I-Phone or I-Pad, he makes an order from Apple etc.

This means that every person needs and will pay for products and services provided by others to live a full- filled life.

3. What is Money?

Money has been defined as a means of payment in the form of metal coins or paper notes. It has also been defined as the legal tender generally accepted within a society, country or nation.

This means that money is what we give in exchange to acquire those things that meet our personal, family and organizational needs.

If what we buy meets our needs, it means it is of value to us. This means money is what we give in exchange for what we value. The latter can be goods or services.

So, from the above, we can see that money can be further defined in two basic ways:

- It is what we give in exchange for things that meet our needs.

- It is what we give in exchange for what is of value to us.

This means that when we give our time and effort to our jobs and receive a salary at the end of the month, we have actually given **money** (i.e. our time and effort) in exchange for **cash** (what we value).

There is an exchange of value on both sides – you

give your time and effort (value), your employer pays you a salary (value) at the end of the month.

The organization is parting with its cash that is of value to them after you have parted with your time and effort which is of value to you.

So, if money is what is used to get value, that means both the salary (cash) and our time and effort can be said to be money.

When we give or use our talents and skills to create a product or service and sell these products and services in exchange for cash, we have actually given our own **kind of money** (i.e. products and services) in exchange for cash.

So, money should not only be seen in terms of cash but in terms of value. That means anything of value is money, provided it can meet the needs of others who are willing to exchange cash, another form of value, for the value you have.

So, real money is not just cash, but value. The reason we need cash is because cash has become the acceptable means of exchange of value across the world.

This is the reason why in the evolution of money, valuable items such as goods and services were not initially exchanged for cash, but for other items of value. This is the concept behind the **trade by barter** system. In this system, many things were used as medium of exchange such as livestock, sacks of cereal grain (shekel), cowry shells or beads and precious metals from which coins were made.

An individual possessing any surplus of value, such as bags of grains or herds of livestock could directly exchange some of it for another form of value such as a clay pot or farm tools.

But the barter system was not efficient because it depended on the "**coincidence-of-wants**" e.g. the seller of food grains has to find a buyer who wants to buy grains and who also could offer in return something the seller wants to buy.

There was no agreed standard measure by which both sellers and buyers could exchange commodities according to the relative value of all the various goods and services offered by other potential barter partners.

In time, coins of copper, silver and later gold, was used as a means of exchange for specific weights of grains, livestock and other goods and services.

These coins soon became too heavy to carry in large quantities and too dangerous to move around because of the activities of robbers – then the paper currency (cash) was born.

Ever since then, cash has been used as a legal tender, a means of exchange for goods and services. People have become so accustomed to cash that they no longer realize that, it's only a means of exchange for the real value of our talents, skills, time, effort and creativity which has been packaged in the form of goods and services.

When we begin to see money not only as cash, but as talent, skill, time, effort and creativity, it shows us the direction we must take, what we must do to have more money if we want to.

If we are desirous of having more money, if we want to have more cash to get the things we want in life, we must be ready to give more and more value to the world.

4. What is Value?

Value can be defined as the usefulness, importance or worth of a thing to an individual. It can also be defined as how desirable a thing is to a person to the extent that it meets the needs or wants, measured by his or her willingness to pay for it.

Value can be a material or monetary one, considered to be a fair exchange in return for a thing; it is the monetary worth of something such as goods or services. It can also be the utility or satisfaction that goods or a service provides.

From the above definitions we the see the following characteristics of value:
- It is based on how useful or important it is to the person concerned.
- It depends on how much an individual desires a thing and whether or not he or she is willing to pay for it.

Despite the fixed monetary value attached to a new car, the sense of value to each person is different. While one person will be willing to pay the market value for the car because he or she really desires to have it, another person may see it as a waste of resources.

If you want money in abundance, you must know how to exchange cash for **real value** or what is called intrinsic value.

Intrinsic value is the actual value of a thing. It is value a thing, such as an asset, is actually worth and the benefit it will provide over the long run, rather than its current market value which can be influenced by speculation.

If you turn your cash to trash buy, using your money to buy things that will continue to take money out of your pocket, you have not exercised a proper judgment of value.

But, if you acquire assets that will continue to be of benefit to you for a long time to come, by continuously putting cash into your pocket, then, you have got yourself a substance of value.

Since the value of cash is consistently on the decline, it is wisdom that when you have acquired it as an exchange of your talent, skills and effort, you also exchange it for assets that have real or intrinsic value.

When the value of the asset you acquire continually puts money in your pocket, then at this point you make **money aka cash** to work for you instead of working for it.

For example, if I work and earn a salary at the end of the month, the salary I receive is the value my employer exchanges for the value of my efforts. It is now my duty to exchange this cash for more value by either investing into a business or buy an asset e.g. a property that will provide me with more cash in the future.

5. The Concept of a Seed

We all know what a seed is, we all know what it looks like. Most of us have used it in our small home gardens and seen the results.

Longman dictionary defines a seed as a small hard object produced by most plants, by which a new plant of the same kind can grow, and which is used for planting.

From the definition above it shows that a seed has four characteristics:

- It is small

- It is produced

- It can cause growth of its kind

- It has to be planted.

i. A Seed is Small

A single seed on its own is small and insignificant. It does no good by itself or for the one who has it. If a single seed is eaten, it cannot satisfy anyone . A single seed cannot be sold to anyone, because no one would buy it. A farmer needs several hundreds and possibly thousands of seeds to grow his crops.

ii. A Seed is Produced

Seeds come from fruits and fruits come from trees or plants. To have seeds, you can only get them from plants or trees that have produced fruits, because fruits have lots of seeds contained in them.

iii. It can Cause Growth of Its Kind

Every seed has the capacity to reproduce itself. It is an inbuilt programme designed by the creator, to work whenever the seed is put into the right soil and given the right nurturing. A mango seed will not produce a guava tree, seeds of rice will not produce a harvest of tomatoes. Whatever the farmer desires to have as his harvest, he must sow the seeds for it.

iv. The Seed Has To Be Planted

With all the valuable characteristics of a seed, it remains dormant and cannot achieve any of its potentials if it is not planted. A seed needs to be planted before its inbuilt program begins to work. It is only when a seed is planted that it can grow up to become a tree that will produce fruits which contains several more seeds in it.

6. Money is a Seed

To be successful with the use of money, to build wealth and have more than enough financial resources required to live that comfortable life you want, you must see and treat money as a seed:

i. Money Starts Small

If you are reading this book, I believe you must have handled money in some way. You must have worked or are working right now, and you are paid a certain amount as salary. The money may look small to you, but that's the point- it is a seed and seeds are meant to be small.

The little money you have left after you have settled all your expenses, will not be very beneficial to you if it is consumed too. On its own, this money cannot not satisfy you because it is a seed and you must see as that.

ii. More Seed Money Will Come From What You Are Doing

The first step to increasing your wealth is to use the money you generate from your current job or business and build on it.

Your current job or business will continue to

provide you with the seed-money you require for investment.

As much as we have heard and seen so many success stories, of those who quit their jobs and started with nothing, it is advisable not to go the same way.

You might not have the stomach to stand up to all the hardships they had to go through. Your best and safest option is to gradually build your wealth from where you are.

iii. Money Invested Produces More of its Kind

Just as a seed can cause the growth of its kind, money can be used to generate more money, and as a matter of fact that is what money should always be used for. Money should not just be consumed or only used to pay for living expenses, it can be and should be grown, and should be increased.

iv. Money Must be Planted

Just like a seed which must be planted into the ground to produce more, money must be planted or invested to have more of it. And just as the right soil is required for the seed to grow, the right investment is required for the money to grow. If you put money into the wrong investment, it can die, just as a seed with all its potentials can die in the wrong soil.

An American Billionaire once wrote: *"Money is like talent. It doesn't do much good if you keep it to yourself. It has to be developed. It has to be nurtured. It has to be used properly. It takes time, work and patience"*

7. Seed-Time and Harvest

Today we are in a world of instant gratification. People want instant success, instant riches and instant wealth. Everybody wants to get rich now, to become wealthy in the shortest amount of time. There are so many online publications, blogs and videos that advertise quick wealth schemes and sell you the idea that you can make so much money in a short period of time.

I once came across online advertorial that promised $15,000 in one week, if you bought their forex trading system software. Since I did not purchase the system, I cannot ascertain for sure if it works or not, but it gives you an idea of the mentality of our time – instant everything.

But this violates the principle of success and life in general. The principle of **seed-time** and harvest is very key to success.

When a farmer plants his seed, he does not expect it to germinate and bear fruit in a week. He knows quite well that the principle of time must be applied on the seed before it can germinate. He knows that after the seed germinates as a plant, it takes time to develop into a grown tree.

The farmer also knows that only after the plant is mature, that is when it begins to produce fruit. All these process take time.

No business can be successful in a day or a month. Some might begin to show signs of success within six months to one year, but every business that will stand the test of time, needs to be developed for a long time.

If you want to be rich and you are not ready to appreciate the value of time, you may truncate the process before the harvest matures.

Before harvest comes, before the profits from the business are reaped, there is a space of time that must go into it. When it comes to investment, time is much more precious than money.

8. Plant Trees Not Crops

There are basically two types of plants we grow for food and they are Crops and Trees. Crops are **non-perennial** plants that are grown for food. They include maize, sorghum, wheat, barley, rice etc. They are called non-perennial plants because they do not live for more than two years.

Trees on the other hand are woody perennial plants that live for many years, sometimes several thousands of years. The oldest known living tree - the **Old-Tjikko** in Sweden is about **9,550 years** old, followed by **Methuselah** in California which is about **5,000** years old.

The oldest living fruit tree is the **Endicott Pear Tree** in Danvers, Essex County, Massachusetts, it is **383** years old.

Differences between Crops & Trees

i. Crop plants produce fruit for a season and then die, while trees produce fruit every season for several years depending on the nature of the tree.

ii. Crops plants do not take long to germinate, grow and bear fruit, while trees take time to germinate, grow and bear fruits.

iii. Crops can be wiped out when attacked by diseases, pests or even drought, but trees have built strong defenses against disease, pests and have deep roots to get their water from inside the ground so they cannot be affected by drought.

9. Invest for the Long Term

When planning for your financial future, you must take time to identify what you are going to invest your money in i.e. is it a **crop investment** or a **tree investment**.

Is the investment just going to yield dividend now and for the next two years, or it will continue to yield dividends that will outlast your lifetime and be there for generations to come.

Your investment view must be long term. You must choose to invest in assets that will continue to generate income for you no matter the economic climate. So for every investment you must make, you have to ask yourself the following critical questions:

i. How long will this investment generate dividends for me?

ii. Will it generate quick cash for me now and not be there tomorrow.

Some investments that could fit into this criteria includes:

i. Real Estate which provides you with rent for life.

ii. Stocks of established companies with a long record of profitable operations and prospects of future growth can provide you with dividends for life.

iii. If you are a writer, you can develop good books that can pay royalties for life.

10. Good Investments Need Time To Grow and Mature

Any good business that is sure to last the test of time, will take time to build. To build a solid house, you must first lay the foundation, build the pillars, raise the blocks add lintel to it and then fix the roof. All these do not happen in day, they take time to put together.

The same apply for a business. To build a solid business that will survive economic shocks and the ups and downs of world economies, the business must continue to grow and this takes time.

One of the reasons why trees survive and last for hundreds and thousands of years is because a new layer of wood is formed within the tree from time to time which makes them grow in diameter.

This layer is called the **annual ring** or **growth ring**. As a new layer is formed, it protects the inner layers from disease and pest attack. As the ring increases, the tree becomes stronger and is able to withstand any external attack. This can only happen after a long time.

Drawing from the wisdom of how a tree grows, to build a business that will survive the hard times, the business must continue to grow and expand. The boundaries of the business must be expanded and pushed forward.

The new business will serve as a ring that will protect the older businesses and the wealth of the company in general. This definitely will take a long time and there are no short cuts, or else the business will be here today and gone tomorrow.

Sir Francis Bacon once wrote – *"He that resteth upon gains, certain shall hardly grow to great riches...."*

If you invest in business that will provide you with income continually for the long term, you will always have income and cash to meet your needs and help others. You will not go broke.

A Very Successful Business Man once wrote: *"Having your own business is like growing a tree. It is a living organism that goes through seasons and storms and beautiful summer days and winter blizzards, but it keeps growing and it's literally and expression of yourself."*

11. You Need the Crops

Crops do have their value. It is crops that feed the world. Farmers cultivate massive acres of land every year to produce food that the world consumes. Most of the staple foods people eat such as rice, maize, sorghum etc. are all crops. For crops to feed the world, they must be produced in mass quantities.

Trees are excellent and they last a long time, but the problem with trees is that they also take a long time to produce tangible fruits. I can say this because the Mango tree I planted in my garden took almost five years to begin to bear good fruit.

The farmer cannot stay hungry waiting for a fruit tree to produce. He may die in the process if there is no alternative to feed him and his family.

So, this is why crops are needed. They can grow fast and feed a lot of people. The same principle should apply to your investments. If you are just starting out in life and a beginner in the world of investing, it will be difficult and be a mistake to get into real estate first, you will not have the resources to do so.

It will be wiser to begin with investments that can generate quick returns for you in the short run, so that in time you can invest in the large businesses.

You need to put your money in a business that can generate immediate cash flow for you to take care of yourself, your family, meet your daily cash needs, give you time to build your cash reserves, improve your business and investment skills, then begin to invest in business or investments that will generate continuous cash flow over the long haul.

Investments that are plants that can generate cash flow for you in the short and medium term include:

i. A new restaurant, bakery, or ice cream outlet.

ii. Your job can be good source of cash flow for the short term. On the job you can learn skills, gain experience that you will require to run your own business.

12. A Tree Does Not Make a Forest

There is a popular African proverb that says – "*A tree does not make a forest*". In real terms this is true. A single tree does not constitute a forest. A forest is made up of several millions of trees, for example, the **Amazon forest** which represents over half of the planets remaining rainforest, is estimated to have **390 billion** individual trees.

But looking at this proverb from another angle, it will not be totally true. A tree can make a forest. A tree that produces fruits and left untouched for several thousands of years can make a forest.

When the fruits of a single tree ripen, they fall to the ground, decay and the seeds in them begin to produce new trees. These trees will grow to maturity and begin to produce their own fruits, which also falls to the ground and generate new trees. If this process is repeated over and over for a very long period of time, you will have a forest.

The wisdom to take from this is that, a single investment is not sufficient for you to have abundance of financial resources. You must continue to make new investments in assets, year in year out to have the financial freedom you desire.

Having just a single investment, no matter how much it is currently generating, is a very risky and dangerous financial position to be in. I can say this from my own personal experience.

A wise investor will continue to move the profits he or she has made from one business venture, and reinvest into new business ventures and do this over and over again. This is what **Warren Buffet** has been doing and continues to do.

13. Prune the Trees

A plant that must grow to its fullest potential must consistently be pruned. Proper pruning is essential in developing a tree with a strong structure and desirable form.

Pruning involves removing dead, damaged and diseased branches to help prevent insect and decay organisms from entering the tree.

This helps to provide more food and water for the tree and stimulate growth in sparse areas of the tree, thereby stimulating the formation of flowers and fruit buds. When a plant is pruned, it grows healthier and produces more fruits.

Some consequences of not conducting a regular pruning programme includes increased risk of whole-tree failure and tree defects which results in poor appearance.

The same applies to business. If you have planted crops or trees, if over time, you have invested in various businesses, you need to constantly evaluate them, find out those that are not doing very well, exit from those businesses and reinvest the money realized into new ventures. This you must do consistently to maintain a healthy investment portfolio.

14. Steps for Successful Investment

i. Save

Firstly, the foundational step required to begin your journey to building your finances, is to save.

To save simply means to keep a specified amount of money and consistently add to it, so that it can be used when the need arises.

This is the basic idea behind savings. It is to keep cash aside, stored in your bank account that will be needed for use on any later date in the future.

If you don't keep aside at least 10% or more of what you earn you will have financial crisis and there is no way you can build your wealth.

As we have seen severally, there are times when the economy of nations slows down, which could be due to a fall in oil prices that have caused a massive drop in the dollars earned by nations, insurgency, war or even political crisis. These situations can cripple the economy of nations.

For example, a powerful nation like China, the manufacturing hub of the world, has experienced a slowdown in its manufacturing output because of weak demand from other parts of the world.

Nations will have no other choice, than to fall back on the cash reserves they have built over time, to augment the shortfall in their budgets. As it applies to countries so it applies to organizations and to individuals.

You have heard of companies declaring bankruptcy and laying off thousands of workers. Companies that have not closed shop have downsized and had terminate services of many employees.

And many people were not ready for this. For those who did not have substantial amount stored in their bank accounts that could carry them through the period when they had no jobs - they were in crisis mode.

With no job and no savings to fall back to, and with a long list of bills piling up to be paid, most sold their cars, and anything of value they had in order to survive. They also lost their homes and some their dignity.

So, to avoid financial crisis you must save.

The amount you keep aside for savings, if done consistently, will begin to cumulatively increase and provide you with the seed or part of the seed required for any future investment.

Thirdly, savings is a means to prevent or avoid waste of resources. There are times during your working career or even in your business life, when you be paid bonuses or have excess cash. At these times there is no need for waste which can be in the form of buying of unwanted items like clothes, electronics, iPads etc.

When you receive such a bonus or have excess cash, you should save it in the bank.

Warrent Buffet's Coach and Mentor, **Benjamin Graham** once wrote – "…..*You might suddenly need to bank your money out of stocks, not 40 years from now* **but** *40 minutes from now ….. Without a whiff of warning, you could lose your job ….. Everyone must keep some assets in the riskless haven of cash"*

ii. Use Your Capital to Invest

If you have noticed, what you could buy with one dollar or one pound three years ago, you can no longer buy with the same amount.

What has happened is that the cash you have in your hands or bank account is losing its purchasing power or buying value i.e. you now need more money to pay for the same amount of goods or services.

There are many reasons for this, but one major factor is constant increase in the prices of goods and services and this is known as *inflation.*

With continuous inflation, it means that the purchasing power will continue to be on the decrease. Anyone still trying to hold on to a fixed dollar income, will face hardships as the cost of living continues to advance.

So, if you stop at just saving your money, its value will continue to erode. So, instead of building your financial base, you will actually continue to deflate it.

One way to counter inflation, one way to mitigate against the effects of continuous rise of goods and services is to grow your cash at a much faster rate than the amount of value it loses daily, weekly monthly or yearly.

For example, let's say that Inflation takes place at a rate of 3% annually, which means that the value of your money stored in the bank is losing its value or purchasing power at 3% annually.

You need to create an asset that will be generating a cash flow of at least 5% per annum, which is more than the amount been lost on your stored value.

You see money is a seed and if a seed remains alone, it is not of much good to anyone. If the seed is consumed, it would not satisfy. If the seed is consumed, there is no hope for tomorrow. For a seed to be useful, for it to feed and satisfy its owner, for it to create a basis for survival and hope for its owner, it must be sown to produce a harvest. When there is a harvest, it will be beneficial not only to owner, but also to other people.

The same with money. If money must become beneficial to its owner and to others, it must be sown or invested. To invest simply means to put money into a particular use, such as a business to make a profit. Profit is simply an increase of the initial amount invested.

15. Point to Note

Using savings to build wealth is a slow process, it takes time. You can increase the speed of your wealth acquisition by using debt to invest in productive ventures, i.e. use debts to acquire assets.

But, like **Robert Kiyosaki** says, debt is like a **loaded gun** which should be handled carefully, if it is in the hands of the wrong person is can be very disastrous.

If you are new to investment, it's safe to start with your own savings or with the savings of those close to you. If there are any challenges with the business or the business goes burst, you won't have to experience the huge anxiety and stress that comes from running around to pay off debt.

If you have had substantial business experience and desire to increase your wealth at a much faster pace, then you can begin to gradually experiment with using debt to acquire assets.

16. Ways to Increase Your Money

There are several types of ways by which the money you have can be increased and they include the following:

i. Business

A business is an activity that involves the buying and selling of goods and services. It can also be defined as any money earning activity or place such as a shop or factory.

Since you may not have the skills, time or experience

to go into business for yourself, I have suggested the following ways by which you can easily go into business.

ii. Partnership

One way to get into a business that can allow you to learn the ropes and avoid the so many pitfalls that entrepreneurs go through in the course of their business life, is to partner with someone who is already in business, is successful at it and he or she is a person you can trust.

This person, if he or she is a person of integrity will open up and guide you through the process. You will easily learn the pitfalls, the challenges and the successes of behind the business.

iii. Network Marketing

This is a very easy way to leverage on an existing established business, its systems, its knowledge, its expertise and make a profit from it.

There are so many network marketing businesses available now for you to choose from. You can register with anyone of them and enjoy the benefits of their trainings, startup kits and people support they provide, to give you the head start you need to make money from their business.

iv. Franchise

This is a special right given or sold to one person or group of people that allows that person or group to sell the company's goods and services in a particular place.

You can buy the franchise rights of an existing successful company e.g. a restaurant chain. This method is easy to hit the ground running making money, but it is also expensive.

v. Intellectual Property

You can write a book and give out the publishing rights to a company. The company will continue to pay you royalties for life. The more books you write the more royalties you get.

Sites like Amazon can offer you monthly royalties based on how many e-books sold or the number of pages of your book read by its subscribed readers worldwide.

vi. Talent or Skill

You can develop your talent or skill to a very high level that the demand for your services will be on the increase. For example, you can develop your teaching or public speaking skills and build a training, coaching or counseling business around it.

vii. Real Estate

You can build houses and rent them out and generate monthly or annual cash flow from rents. This method is capital intensive and slow, but if made on a consistent basis, real estate is one **"tree"** type of investment that will give you cash flow for life.

viii. Business

You can setup a business of your own after you have learnt the ropes. Most times the best way to start your business is to offer services that are in line with your skills and talent.

For example, if you know how to cook, you can start a restaurant business. If you are good at making fantastic hair-dos, you can start a hair styling business, and if you have a passion for fashion, you can setup a fashion house.

After you have done this for a while or a few years, you can step it up by expanding the business to various locations.

17. Auto Pilot

There is a level to which you build your assets and your finances to and they begin to run on auto pilot. This means you have created enough assets that generate cash flowing into your hands daily, weekly and monthly, that, you don't have to work another day for money.

This means that though you still continue to work, at this time you are not working to earn more money but working to achieve the goals you want and you are not under any pressure to survive.

It means that even if you go to sleep for a few days or fall sick or become indisposed, you will still have enough money flowing in to take care of your expenses.

18. Improving Your Financial Knowledge

Robert Kiyosaki in his books, emphasizes the need for continuous financial education and I cannot agree with him more.

John Maxwell once wrote *"knowledge alone does not make you a leader, but without it you cannot become one"*

Those who have made tremendous advances in life, were men of knowledge, not necessarily men who had more formal education, but men he knew what others did not know.

They seem to have developed an unending fascination with new knowledge and in time discovered hidden wisdom that was not common place to others, applied that wisdom and it moved them far ahead of their peers.

The same goes for money and success in general. If you want to be successful and stay successful in a fast changing world, you must continue to update your financial knowledge.

The tragedy of life is when a man comes to a point in his life when he thinks he has known it all and has nothing more to learn.

Even a PHD holder in economics, knows that he or she has not ready all the books of economics ever written or will he ever be able to read them all in his life time.

This means that there is always room to know more and improve on what you already know.

The same goes for money and financial knowledge in general. If you want to have more money you must know more about money. You must continue to strive to educate yourself financially every passing day, no matter how much wealth you have or how much you already know.

Financial risk really does not lie in the kind of

investment an individual invests in, but in the individual himself. If he does not continue to update himself financially, he will continue to take poor financial decisions that will lead to loss of capital invested.

Benjamin Graham once wrote – *"The kind of securities (stocks) to be purchased and the rate of return to be sought depend not on the investor's resources but on his financial equipment in terms of knowledge, experience and temperament"*

Bill gates has been described as a **voracious reader** and he is always on the search for new knowledge to break into new frontiers.

To become wealthy and keep yourself in that place, you must daily search for new financial wisdom to add to what we already know.

You must read new books, listen to more tapes, attend more seminars and continue to improve your financial wisdom.

I used to be scared of debt, because of all the humiliation I went through when I was in debt and did not want to go through it again, until I read **Robert Kiyosaki's** book on **Improving Your Financial IQ**.

In it I discovered how you can use debt to your

advantage, buy investing debt in productive ventures that will produce more cash flow, instead of using debt to buy luxuries.

This is the power of knowledge. Overtime the concept of money, how it is made and lost has undergone an evolution, if we do not evolve with it we would be found wanting.

Up till this day and throughout my life time, I will be on the constant search for new financial wisdom to add to what I already know, because learning is an investment.

Remember the words of **Einstein** – *"The mind that opens up to a new idea never comes back to its original size."*

Keep learning, keep growing, keep improving your financial wisdom and you will continue to have more to live the life you have always dreamed of.

19. On a final note

"It requires a great deal of boldness and a great deal of caution to make a great fortune; and when you have got it, it requires ten times as much wit to keep it" – **Nathan Mayer Rothschild.**

ABOUT THE AUTHOR

Mr. Vincent Hope Okoh is a graduate of Mathematics Education and a very experienced Educator with over twenty (20) years of Teaching, Instructing and Training Experience.

He is an author of several academic and non-academic books among which are "My Leadership Collections", "The Aisle", "The Story of My Mother", "Deeper Secrets of Wealth" etc.

He is an Entrepreneur, Management Expert and Leader, having lead his own company from an unknown position to an ICT firm of repute that has trained so many individuals in various ICT Skills, who are currently employed in different sectors of the economy.

He is happily married to Mrs. Deborah Nanchin Vincent and they are blessed with three beautiful daughters Angel, Joy and Anita.